Air Circus

PIANOSTOOL
FOOTNOTES

Simon cutts

THE
JARGON SOCIETY
1982

Library of Congress Catalog Card No: 82-83361

ISBN: 0-912330-55-4 (paper)
ISBN: 0-912330-54-6 (cloth)

Manufactured in Great Britain by
Titus Wilson & Son Limited,
Kendal, Cumbria, England

Designed by Simon Cutts and Jonathan Williams

Distributed by
Inland Book Company,
22 Hemingway Avenue,
East Haven, Connecticut 06512, USA
Telephone: (203) 467-4257

for Margot

Piano   stool   foot   notes

Jargon 94

Jardins sous la pluie

The arabesque parade
    of umbrellas and gardens
in the rain
whose flowers are unmentioned
    in their colours
the town is so grey

moonshine and
daybreak

two caravans
parked

end to
end

Pour remercier la pluie au matin

in Devonshire Park

the sensation is minute
of rain disturbing

fountain boats

of silver rain
dries with a

a roof mottled
within minutes

passing train
by the factory

the wind chime
jammed
by thunder

cords
tangled
by gales

tuneless
on loose
knots

Pails of Weather

The tower has dissolved, producing mushrooms
which rise only intermittently from the small
islands in the lake

Cumulus St. is ten kilometers long and exists
from time to time on days when there are moderate
winds

Shepherd's Pie

The open sea. When the sea drifts inland over
warm ground, along the promenade, the clouds
are shred into dried air. The sands

Pillow cases seen low in the sky from a distance
seem very slim because they are nearly edge on.

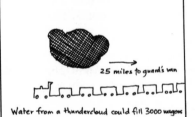

25 miles to guard's van

Water from a thundercloud could fill 3000 wagons

The streetlamp's custard
falls at tea-time.

The chief portion of Prof. Espy's theory*
has been anticipated by Francis Bacon:

"There is no exquisite beauty
without some strangeness
in proportion"

—ce qu'a vu le vent d'Ouest.
Reich too had an explanation for it!

* *Of Storms, Boston 1841*

Flags upon
the weather map
indicate a plot

forming off
Gris Nez

in the shape
of a trough

Weather

Microturbulence on the surface
of waters
and rime from waterfall spray

a storm-glass cannot measure

skin
so
soft

sky
so
thin

the braid of a bird's
footpath in the snow.

late starlings

startled
by traffic

resettle

Between reproductions
it already turns season

on the white
magpie whose pigments

are shadow

twigs are scarce
in the air where

whimbrel and godwit
inhabit the occasional

gorse of the foreshore

camouflage silhouette

magpie

o the bandage
of the route

the sling between
hills

the white
shoot

pebble
ripple

ripple
pebble

pebble

ripple

scarce
      sparce
spruce
      larch

a pebble
out

of its
hole

on fallow
ground

Clare's 'Journey Out of Essex'

a brief transcription

having only
myself

in my army
I
led the way

an old
wide awake
hat

and a plum
pudding
bonnet

in my
pocket

another of those
broken down
haymakers

I lay
down by

a shed
under

some elms

here I am
homeless
at home

and happy
anywhere

hill song

solo
echo

**After Samuel Palmer's version
of Virgil's 'Eclogues'**

folding
the flock

open-
ing the
fold

fold-
ing the
last

sheep

for Stephen D

whose hoofs have
trampled near
the clôche

lost in the spent
stick bonfire's last

bundles of smoke
from the plot

This guide book
printed in the Midlands
still applies to Rye

whose windmill sails
remain nailed up to
show it does not go

Moulin à vent:
Windmill for Sail

The Dutch Fruit Economy

clogs
windmill cogs
apple logs
apples

apple ladder
windfall trolley

At Sea

What could the boy
hope to draw,

the lines of his
exercise book

going the other
way, and anyway

the same view
had not changed

since yesterday

I neither hear
nor see nor
feel the sea

Les Enerves de Jumièges

as the blanket
absorbs

water, bunk
by bunk

the raft
submerges.

The four-
poster

set
sail.
The pier

Having a lovely time.

The sea is outside
one side

of our caravan.
Hope you have no more
of that toothache trouble.

love Mam

I prefer the streams
of the mountain
to the sea

Mr G. White of Messrs Green & White

the name of a wave in a sea of waves

All his life Mr. S. Mills
has been trying to say
something exactly arbitrary
about the sea.

The Fallaway Promenade

the sea, permanent waved

yachts

occasionally
stationary

Sail Toil

Soil Sale

Thro' the ilôts
of shadows
of the sky's
white pillows

the silhouettes
of nets
little boats
sail between

The spiritsail   is
barge with   able
its flat   to go
bottom-   whenever
ed hull   there is
                a heavy
         fall of dew

A letter rack

the paper clip
anchors

the boat.
A sail
of the envelope

Trompe l'Oeil

Listen to a bucket
of flowers;

an ear trumpet

Family

Lily is in
the water.
Iris is not

$$\frac{LSY}{S}$$

Flower

a word we have used

the *e* is petalled
by memory

Rosé

Dufy

Based upon the broken
Fruitstall

The hill,
colours of aquarelle.

The immobile sale of flowers

L.McC

Watercolours replenished.

A vase
of flowers
changes

by fading

Poinsettia

my favourite flowers are leaves

a paisley

for Tom

cowslip
clover &
parsley

Wisteria

streamers

in continuous
blueness

out of the blue

of the chestnut blossom
on the roof
of the dustbin lorry

rain bowl
rose

rose bowl
rain

The Illustrated Garden

a taste of
fresh linen
turned into kidneys

of fold
by a breeze
the window

is open in.
The tissue of skin

a pencil leaves

across the path,
the bed.

A bandage
of soft

plumage

Blossom

the blotting
paper behind

the crockery
cabinet
window

has faded.
Its dust
leaves

a perfume
of furniture
cream

on the corduroy
tablecloth

the cake crumbs
are hidden

in furrows
of moss

the breeze
lifts
the tablecloth

the rain
washes
the plates

these cakes
are kept
under glass

and their
crumbs

swept off
the grass

affection
confection

cakes
confetti

after Morandi

a shadow
of fluted
cake paper
wavers

in the kitchen
garden,

the cups
have exploded

and buds
of magnolia

are hooked
on the tree

sills
sunken
in leaves.

puddles

Duplicate
sink gardens

continuous or
occasional

Sundial

An orchard at Stonypath

h'arbour
d'apple

A tree-seat at Windyhill

the cupboards
at each
end held

windfalls

stored
for winter
in drawers

Topiary

the variegated
tail

of the privet.
Aeroplane

Topiarists 1-5

I

The topiarist builds
umbrellas,
anvils, loaves

and later discovers
crumbs on the floor

nails in the lawn
and sequins on the road

2

Holes through the hedge
are wire outlines
surrounding

Breakages, as
buttonholes

are tears
inside silk

Shrinkages

3

Snuff
in his
turnups

Lawns
full
of confetti.

A biscuit
tin lid
full

of leaves

4

Several other
dampsquibs

in the greenhouse
and shrubbery

misfire
simultaneously.

5

A scarecrow's
pocketful
of sparrows:

his squadrons
of swallows

teapot topiary
airport aviary

meringues

in
the Snowman's
pipe.

white.
coke Buttons.

Garden Warfare

sunken
harbour

garden

sunken
garden

harbour

aircraft
carrier

bag

aircraft

carrier
bag

Glyders

the delicate petticoat
of an aeroplane wing
wrinkles the shade

of a fusilage wind;
Hems of clock propellers

The First Aeroplane, 1903

He will take off
if the weather is safe
and land
in a field on his chair
with no legs,
sliding a good distance.

Les coquelicots

after the last greenhouse,
the airfield

the vague ness
of long

poppy-grass

Frottage

the phantasy
is anchored

by a gnome
in the garden

The Blind Garden

the braille chairs
lie about
the flowers;

the petals
and the prickle
of the rhododendron

or the rose?

Golliwog's Cake Walk

Dear Sir could you tell me
whether the crazy
is pathment or paveway

icy
   crazy
paving
     ivy

Winchelsea

Gnomes in
the gardens
of railway
carriages

corrode
to corset
pink.

Chipped
plaster eye
brow and

wheelbarrow
to alabaster
cauliflower

Chronicles of a Garden Railway

Instead of strike
and go-
slow,

read: snow
and rain

stop-play.

I had not
noticed
before, but

Grace
batted
in brogues.

Along the crease
trailed
an undone
lace.

O brown
shoe
leather

& oiled
willow

and now we have
Snow again

from the pavilion
end

as a train moves
into the Warwick Rd
statïon without
stopping

the pitch
a little dew
in it
still

Rooks nest
on the pitch

in the holes
of the net

of the hockey
club's goals.

le Water-ski

Collapses

into
the water
in a dusty

packamac

clouds washing
blossom

clouds
blossom washing

Clouds

of vapour
formed

as drapery

Bateau-en-Ciel

a bush of clothes
you wear in the wind

built of curls

plein de la mer

wind

string vest
socks

string
wind vest

socks

Pedro

From his cliff top allotment
he fishes into a cradle of rock.

His washing smells of smoked
sardines, as do his socks.

the breeze fills
the sleeve
of a shirt

dyeless
and faded
through work

pinafore
pianoforte

petticoat

I feel sentimental
about the dishcloth.

Some underpants
you bought in Bognor.

Leçon

half-a-rainbow
in our playground

Opal sun
in a book
of May

for Karl T

a bedspread
whose hems
gather

the stains
of puddles

from water
colour

window boat

the galleon
whose drapes

fall as lace
on the lake

1

the dull bloom
of polish on
the piano lid.

Light blanches
the ivory keys

2

reflections

in the lid
of a piano

rinsed
by moonlight

On parquet
sunlight

solidifies
its polished

petals

the mantelpiece's
mauve

ovals replace
the goldfish

tailpiece
in the fireplace

Waddington's

even the blinds
are prints

amidst

landscapes,   1
lampshades   2

landscape[1]
(lampshade)

lampshade[2]
(landscape)

Bloembollen

A bouquet
of lampshades
by a canal

Dew on
the barge's
balcony

the tenderness
of two twisted
sweet papers

on Ella Grainger's
dressing table

the oak
mantelpiece

or skirting
board

warp

the deck or
Direc
-tor's chair

still life, after Cézanne

the slow clock
on the shelf
with no hands
continues
to go

for Tom & Laurie

thanks for
the poems

wrapped
in knitting

patterns
and packets

of seaweed
tablets

Chintz Civilisation

One afternoon
China melted
into the tea

the duster makes
a little disaster
amidst

the disused
tea service

in the war
games room

several
helicopters

have landed
near

the biscuit
jar

the balsa
delta

glides
to the armpit

of a sofa

**Concerning Herbert Bayer's
1,000,000 mark bank note, 1928**

a suitcase full
to buy
an egg.

A handbag
full of bus
tickets

Solos, Duets & Quartets for Gris

solace
shoelace

flambes
larmes

(T. Pear
 P. Tear)

egg plant
bread fruit

haberdashery

knapkin &
knapsack

hanky or
doilly

I dislike
the texture of
your lucky dip

with its prizes
the same
as the rubbish

Dear Santa

please send me
a steam
curling

wand or
tong

**Translation of an unwritten
poem by Max Jacob**

The man with the solid
flag

What has he got
in his hat?

All the billets
of return
passengers

in couchettes
in tiers
over his ears.

What a weight
on the taps.

Snap

Ken has a sense of
the ornament. The glamour
of his garden stems from
an aluminium flamingo.

He calls his house
'Morn Mist' because
he always has
the kettle on.

Ice   Berg   Scholar   Ship

Maidenhair

florets
          of dew
in the beard

———————————————————————————————————

"When the pinnae have fulfilled their mission they fall and leave the rachis black and bare. It must have been the sight of a plant from which most of the pinnae had fallen, leaving a shock-head of stiff wiry stalks, that suggested the name of 'Mayden's Heare', but if so the medieval maidens must have been very untidy!"

—Edward Step, F.L.S., *'Wayside and Woodland Ferns'*. 1908

o

banjo
in limbo

Hamish Maclaren's book *'Sailor with Banjo'* was almost completely destroyed by a fire at the warehouse of Victor Gollancz, the publisher, shortly after its appearance in 1929. Thereby, a fine lyric talent was arrested, evidenced only by his own very battered copy of the book, a proof bulging with additional clippings from *'The Observer'*, *'The Spectator'* and *'Radio Times'*.

on the pegboard
cupboard
pelmet,

a hat basket.
The rocker's
ploughshare

blades are
strengthened
by matchwood

staves

On March 8th 1976, I received a postcard from archivist Jean Brown, of the Elder's room in the Shaker House at Hancock, Massachusetts. A reply for her.

Small packets
must

be tied
with bows

not knots

Information given to me by the Post Office upon enquiry as to the true nature of the Small Packet.

cf. Stéphane Mallarmé: *'Les Loisirs de la Poste'*

Someone, some
where

is hammering
formica
to a piano

with a spanner

At 237a Camberwell New Road, London SE5, to be precise, where New Road Bargains had their head-quarters.

a postcard from an acquaintance, of Harry Ramsden's famous fish and chip restaurant near Guiseley in Yorkshire.

over-
      leaf
for lunch

one May
day

_____

Within weeks of the completed renovations to 233 Camberwell New Road, London SE5, the Coracle Press premises, dampness threatened. In a sense, it is permanently autumn at that address, as the property is so old we are constantly unable to surmount the decay. It is also a problem for the watercolours.

the leaves
of burnt
paint
curl

already
the wire
wool turns
rusty

". . . Albers, hopeful that English could be reduced to the logic of German, decided that 'future' had to mean the opposite of 'pasture' . . ."

Martin Duberman. *'Black Mountain: An Exploration in Community.'* p. 45

a pastoral

The future
and pasture

of Arthur
the autist

Tokens of gold, left by us
Are all
There is of You.
So old, the ivy has grown
into a tree
About an house built to Thy mind.

La Mort de Baldassare Silvande

I arrange myself to die, alter
the coverlets.
There through the curtains, a Tea ship
is sailing for India.
Ah! the chime of the distant village
imperceptable and profound as a heartbeat.

Music sheet and violin
will become antique.
The jests they were for me
when the Estate was damp
and rain fell,
have no bearing now.

M.D.

His morality is threadbare.
He prefers chess to all else.
Even his best friend
he lets impersonate him.

Vanity is his one
weakness, or he
would have left
the world, years ago.

The Movement

Surprisingly, only one died
of drink: Bataille; only one
went mad: Artaud;
only one committed suicide:
Crevel; only one was homosexual:
Crevel again; as far as we know.

The Architecture of Russian Orthodoxy

"There is no over
-all plan."

Each man
builds
what
he feels.

Building
a new hang-
over
every day.

In Memorium T.E.H.

the lights
on the crane

jib form
a new

constellation

will the lady
who left
the imitation
snake skin
vanity case
in the cafeteria
please come to
the guards van

for Richard Wilson

a dove-tail

of threadbare
detail;

Eyelets
tied where
wire

& twine
replace
string

Mixed Media Hazard

Take a hammer
and make
your autobiography

A Courtauld Institute Fairy Tale

Albert was cured
of illness by
a beautiful landscape

Courtauld Institute snack

the little bit
of amyl
acetate

in the banana
keeps you awake

dilute the sky with care
and add the pearl
to blue

white blotting paper
absorbing surplus moisture

Sans Mot

Volume of monotone, meets
l'oreille de porcelaine: Night

Matisse completes

a paper
counterpane

for the bed

A Parisian American Arranges Art to Music

Whistler

Rouen

a crust

of calcium
on the façade

of a snail

Degas detested the discomforts
of painting 'out of doors'

"le peintre ce n'est pas du sport"

A studio-creature, the racehorse

permanent Sunday
twilight invades
Hampstead

o dovecôte

.

Trois Morceaux en Forme de Poire

1

Le poire
pour boire.

Un pourboire

2

The graceless
Mock-Turtle exists
only as soup.

3

a brancusi
head
on the piano
lid

A note for Jonathan on his 50th birthday, overheard on the Southampton to Cherbourg ferry

will all members
of the High Wycombe
Youth Orchestra

please meet
their conductor
outside

the sweet-shop
on C deck

petit air

between the blades
of the reed

and the mouthpiece
shallot,

no-gap

t
i

t
s
i

piano
patchwork

guitar
quiltwork

oil
piano
lamp

Scriabin

bird-brain

Fou Ts'ong

I had never heard
a pianist
cough,

his hair cut
to look rough.

The fumes
of his toothpaste
were too strong,

and he had
rather bad

Dandruff

Fauré

the delicacy
of tangerine

marmalade

étincelant
par le vent:

a symphony or
movement

by Debussy

déjà-vu

the wind siffles
pages

of a book
in the garden

whilst butterflies
augment

the sensation
of leaves

Quelques Pianos

a piano of print
shapes
the white air

the gesture
of letters
We cannot hear

A table is too jointed
to enter.

the Piano
rests in a cupboard of its own

without moving
from the shape of a window
making no note without

thinking of Her in polytone.

"Develope a precise foot technique
depressed, shallow in the use
of the forte pedal.

Chopin instructs without
these laurel leaves,
like punctuation in grammar."

Claire de lune

In a Hollywood
pasteboard moon,
a klieg is focused
by a machinist

—the novel introduction
of C♭

(a lovely breeze
and countless shadows
are difficult feelings
for music)

*"The later Beethoven on the new
Bechstein etc."*

So many false
endings
amongst which

"the hills rejoice like lambs"
and begin again.

The bland harmony

You are clever
   can cross over
hands in the space
   of a blank,
and your fingers
   make an elaborate
mime, shuffling
   your pick
into order.
   It's a game
you are playing
   on the domino
keys of
   your harpsichord.

Pour le piano

Fingers that pull hammers
onto strings

Look what I can do with
emotion
with this piece of

Cheese

The Steinway is prepared.
Your accidental playing
will force a chord
into the back room, where
under stairs, reproduction engineers

watch for the pedal

To a musician

    At the beginning of your sarabande,
Light changes around us. The bird in its cage
    Remains still, only its mirror and bell
Disturbs our attention to the bars
    and stress of your four-movement piece.
Even our child's sticky hands do not
    Damage the sound of your piano, whose
Tone seems too magnificent to belong to our room,
    Where we have never had a piano.
After the crescendo on the last track,
    We decided to buy another of your records.

Scores of concertinas
and stairs

Footnotes

The subjects of these pianostools in the following order, were taken from the listed books and pamphlets:

Weather, Birds, Landscape, The Sea, Boats, Flowers, Gardens, Topiary, Aeroplanes, Sport, Washing, Furniture, Domestic Trivia, Art, Music, & Pianos.

Thirteen Preludes	Tarasque Press	1966
Claude Monet in His Water Garden	Tarasque Press	1967
Balcon Programme	Gallery Ten	1967
Camouflage	Gallery Ten	1968
The Blue Boat Train	Tarasque Press	1968
Thoughts to Music	Gemma Three	1970
A New Kind of Tie: Poems 1965-68	Tarasque Press	1972
The Allies	Simon Cutts	1974
A Book of Braids	Coracle Press	1975
leafmould	Coracle Press	1975
Treacle Sandwich Flagpole; Poems 1968-75	Coracle Press	1975
Les Enerves de Jumièges	Aggie Weston's	1975
The Embroidered Topiarist	Coracle Press	1975
Quelque Pianos	Jargon	1976
Mackintosh Buttons	Sarum Press	1976
Clare's Journey	Moschatel Press	1976
Topiarist 3	Coracle Press	1977
Iceberg Scholarship	Circle Press	1978

Monotones	Coracle Press	1978
Waddington's	Coracle Press	1979
Pins	Simon Cutts	1980
Solos, Duets & Quartets	Moschatel Press	1981
Caravanserai	Coracle Press	1981
Pails of Weather	Coracle Press	1981
PG Tips	Coracle Press	1981

[1] Pierre Lalo reviews Debussy's *'La Mer'* at the Concerts Lamoureaux. *Le Temps*, Oct 16 1905

[2] Luminais. *'Les Enerves de Jumièges'*, Musée des Beaux Arts, Rouen.

[3] *Guantanamera*: lines 1-3.

[4] G. Seurat. *'Flôtte à pêche, Port-en-Bessin'*.

[5] *'Je dis: une fleur! et, hors de l'oubli où ma voix relègue aucun contour, en temps que quelque chose d'autre que les calices sus, musicalement se lève, idée même et suave, l'absente de tous bouquets'*. Stéphane Mallarmé.

[6] Bux, Drury Hill, Nottingham, 1967-69.

[7] Stonypath, Dunsyre, Lanarkshire, Scotland. The home and garden of the poet Ian Hamilton Finlay. As yet the orchard does not exist*.
(*1976)

[8] Windyhill, Kilmacolm; designed by Charles Rennie Mackintosh in 1900. The tree-seat no longer exists.

[9] A celebration of the author's construction* in the collection of R. D. Brown.
The Topiarist, 1976.

[10] *'Sports et Divertissements'*, No. 22?

[11] Georges Lemmen. *'Washing'*, 1888.

[12] for Annira.

[13] Edward Hopper 1882-1967.

[14] *'. . . Just the kind of silly 'iceberg' scholarship (more below the footnote than above it) that I rhetorically scorn . . .'*
Martin Duberman. 'Black Mountain: An Exploration in Community', p. 80. E. P. Dutton & Co., Inc., New York, 1972.

[15] T. E. Hulme's poem *'The Man in the Crow's Nest'* was of empirical importance to the Imagists.

[16] The problem for art remains how to draw a bend in a river so that it doesn't seem like a rabbit warren.
'Allotments'. Tarasque Press 1970.

[17] Ford Madox Brown. *'An English Autumn Afternoon'*, 1852-54.

[18] At Kettle's Yard, Cambridge, at the time of H.S. 'Jim' Ede's curatorship, and after.

[19] A Chinese flute with six holes, one covered by an onion-skin membrane producing a nasal tone.

[20] Oil piano lamps added to Percy Grainger's childhood piano.

> *"Two hands*
> *a box-full*
> *of hammers*
> *& strings"*.

[21] *'One has a perfectly sincere craving for a work of art. The work of art may be a Velasquez, a vase by Satsouma, or a New Kind of Tie'*. Claude Debussy. Letter to Prince Poniatowski, February 1893.

[22] *'Pianos are furniture'*. Hugh Creighton Hill.

[23] Separated from the road by a small garden is the room of a house in Rue Nicholet. The hand at the piano is that of Paul Verlaine's mother-in-law, Madame Mauté de Fleurville, pupil of Chopin, and who will give lessons to the young Claude Debussy.

> *"What Saint-Saens says about the use of the pedal in Chopin, is not, despite my respect for his venerable age, altogether correct, for I have precise recollections on the subject from Madame Mauté de Fleurville. Chopin wished his works to be practised without pedal, with but very rare exceptions. This is, moreover, the art of making the pedal a sort of breathing apparatus, which I observed in Liszt's playing. . . . Theoretically one should find some means of showing the 'breathing' graphically."*

Claude Debussy. Pourville, September 1915.

[23a] I would like to thank Thomas Meyer for his patient grouping and selecting of these poems during the early summer of 1981.
Simon Cutts, Aug. 22nd 1982

24 The organ occupies all six rooms of his cottage. The three-manual console is located in a back room and the pipes are to be installed in the roof. In addition to the pipe-work, the organ will produce such sounds as cello, flute, clarinet, drums, cymbals, triangle, carillon, chimes, tom-tom, sleigh bells, oboe, birds, aeroplane, siren, surf and bicycle.

TRAVELLER'S REST PUBLIC HOUSE
In the lounge every Wednesday
JACK FRENCH
at the piano
and at the
Cold Table on Fridays

26 Welte-Mignon's piano roll was the earliest effective recording system and one which must have involved a good deal of mystery, for in order to hear a replay of the roll, the piano had to be vacated whilst it turned itself into a musical box, and the keys of the Steinway, for which the device was prepared, went their own way.

27 Following Welte-Mignon's invention, the gramophone has become a popular piece of furniture.

The Boat

A word has no easy means of representing the thing it must stand for. Least of all does it gain representative significance in the functional use of language which is our habit. For the narrator's words depart at a constant tangent to the boat he describes, which remains placid and static, and is a model of our would-be intentions

The word is in its plainest sense and is not an idea. It remains content and enjoyed in the artifact of representation, the word, as the boat itself can be enjoyed as an artifact of motif or subject.

The Train

A word has no easy means of representing the thing it must stand for. Least of all does it gain representative significance in the functional use of language which is our habit. For the narrator's words depart at a constant tangent to the train he describes, which remains placid and static, and is a model of his would-be intentions.

The word is in its plainest sense and is not an idea. It remains content and enjoyed in the artifact of representation, the word, as the train itself can be enjoyed as an artifact of motif or subject.

The Boat-train
— the train which leaves Victoria Station in exact time to catch the awaiting boat at Dover.
The Boat-train retrieves a substantial ambiguity by reference to an object of ambiguous shape, rather than to an idea. The semantic ambiguity then plays inside the contextual useage of language which for the most part has no concrete basis.

Blue

Adjectival useage has so diminished the positivity of the word 'blue' that in the syntactical arrangement of things, it must always take a second place. The sky is at least as blue as it is sky. That the sky is blue is at least as important as it is sky. Although here part of a sentence, 'blue' is at least as equally unrelated in any absolute sense as 'sky'. Blue's claim, therefore, is to be considered as positive and autonomous as the noun. For eventually we bequeath on the world human condition, by this relegation of 'blue' to a constantly descriptive position. The need to describe then has incurred the reflective condition of the narrator.

An aspect of grammatical association here illustrates the desire to unconditionally modify the world, whereas an equally strong case can be made for the recognition of an independent world, at the side of which all human reflection is its own self-enclosing system of artifice.

It may be true that we have no evidence of the world's existence beyond the narrator's description. But the disciplinary simplicity of assumed objects by which we gain order is an invaluable process. The world then exists to be ordered, not modified in essence; soul is avoided.

And although it can only be of aesthetic importance that we keep clean this ordering, it essentially corresponds to the formal correctness which begins or ends — as soon as we flaw the page.

I

Should Whale-flesh be eaten as fish or as meat?

Whale Goulash

Allow about a quarter of a pound of meat to a person. The cost at the fishmonger's is 1/10 per lb. Cut finely a similar weight of onions and cook in hot fat until they are transparent, but do not allow them to brown. Cut the whale into small cubes, season with salt and sweet paprika, and add it to the onions. Add tomato ketchup to flavour and colour. Keep covered and simmer. Serve with macaroni or dumplings.

Mr. White enjoys his whale. It cuts like beef steak and has the same flavour with just a taste of fish about it. The lack of fat is the drawback in the opinion of some. A dish of whale and chips goes down very nicely thank you.

And the Lord Mayor ate his whale and said: "Let us have it again tomorrow".

2

Are Earthquakes Weather?

If out of doors, keep away from trees, haystacks, houses, large sheets of water, etc. If in the open plain, where there are no trees or buildings, you are safer lying down than standing up. If near a wood, stay there and do not go nearer.

If you are near a single tall tree, you are pretty safe thirty yards away. If you are indoors, hang up a hammock by silken cords, get in, and stay there. Failing a hammock, sit on a chair in the middle of the room with your feet on another, first placing beneath you a feather bed or hair mattress. But do not sit under the chandelier. Whether indoors or out keep away from the chimney.

3

Do Bats Nest?

?

This edition of 1000 copies is set in Garamond types
and printed on Clan Book Wove.
950 copies are bound in paper wrappers. The remaining
50 copies are hand bound in paper over boards,
signed by the author, and numbered 1 through 50.   /50